Blessed Assurance

A couple seek God's protection for their unborn child – and discover hope in the midst of suffering.

Simon Makuyana

O&U
Onwards & Upwards

Onwards and Upwards Publishers
4 The Old Smithy, London Road, Rockbeare,
EX5 2EA, United Kingdom.
www.onwardsandupwards.org

Copyright © Simon Makuyana 2022

The moral right of Simon Makuyana to be identified as the author of this work has been asserted by the author in accordance with the Copyright, Designs and Patents Act 1988.

All rights reserved.

No part of this publication may be reproduced or transmitted in any form or by any means, electronic or mechanical, including photocopy, recording or any information storage and retrieval system, without permission in writing from the author or publisher.

First edition, published in the United Kingdom by Onwards and Upwards Publishers (2022).

ISBN: 978-1-78815-898-5
Editor: Sheri Newton
Typeface: Sabon LT

The views and opinions expressed in this book are the author's own, and do not necessarily represent the views and opinions of Onwards and Upwards Publishers or its staff.

Unless otherwise specified, Scripture quotations are from The Authorized (King James) Version. Rights in the Authorized Version in the United Kingdom are vested in the Crown. Reproduced by permission of the Crown's patentee, Cambridge University Press.

Scripture quotations marked (NLT) are taken from the Holy Bible, New Living Translation, copyright © 1996, 2004, 2007, 2013 by Tyndale House Foundation. Used by permission of Tyndale House Publishers, Inc., Carol Stream, Illinois 60188. All rights reserved.

Contents

Introduction 1
1. Breaking Waters 4
2. Blessed Assurance 10
3. Pregnancy and the Awaited News 18
4. A Test of Faith 24
5. Learning to Trust God 30
6. The Cost of Obedience 35
7. Finding the Holy Spirit's Comfort 43
8. Birth 50
9. Unplugged? 60
10. Avery's Legacy 68
11. Did God Answer Our Prayers? 73

Dedication to Avery 79
About the Author 80

Introduction

One fateful morning in kindergarten, I was asked to sing alone, and my voice decided to bail out on me. This led the teachers to call each other and examine the inside of my mouth, trying to discover if there was something wrong with my voice box. They did not see anything, but one of the teachers was sure something was medically wrong. On that day, I was sentenced to never sing again in my life. This did not only end any potential singing career but from that day onward, I became self-conscious, recoiling in self-protection from every opportunity for public speaking, and that led to the development of other negative attributes in my character including shyness and perfectionism. I became so sensitive to whatever was wrong with my voice box, along with other aspects of my life, because I did not want another episode of humiliation in front of the other children in my class, much less in front of an audience. I was so bright in school, but I became notorious for not wanting to share ideas. I never raised my hand when the teacher asked a question, and would only answer when asked directly. No one ever noticed that I needed help.

My kindergarten teachers diagnosed me in my presence and in the company of other children, but never did a follow-up with my parents. The diagnosis might have been made in error, but I had heard it. My first mistake was to believe it, and my second mistake was not to do anything about it. Soon enough, it led to a self-fulfilling prophecy.

However, later in life, tired of shying away from opportunities to speak up and be heard, I embarked on a quest for self-development. I discovered that God designs some burdens for you to bear on your own for a purpose in life. He lets you take an active role in seeking solutions, with Him directing your feet to the answers you desperately desire. This is designed to strengthen you and help you develop your character just like the process behind a butterfly breaking free from its cocoon. Before emerging from its cocoon, a butterfly will strengthen its wings by beating them against the inside. If you were to help free it from the cocoon, you would prevent its wings developing the strength they need for survival. In other words, you would cut short its life.

This book tells the story of my daughter Avery. The trials my family experienced were again like a cocoon. We didn't know how our daughter or we would emerge – and often God seemed silent while we tried to make sense of everything happening. But ultimately, our understanding of 'blessed assurance' would grow, and we would discover great hope and comfort.

We did not come through the journey without some scars, however. Traumatic experiences can challenge your assumptions about the world – about the way the world works, about what you can expect in life and even about God's ways. But the scars from those experiences leave you wiser and able to make better choices going forward, and so better equipped to face the world. They can ultimately deepen your relationship with God.

Permit me to share with you both the scars in my life as I uncover them one by one and the secret of my ability to remain calm and steadfast amid trials. I invite you to see what the

Introduction

Lord has consistently done for me and how He has magnificently worked through supernatural and natural means. As I have reflected on my life, I can see with even more clarity how in His providence God has often permitted the fires of affliction to assail me that I may be purified for His glory. Like limping Jacob, I might bear scars, but not without His blessings.

As you read my story, my desire is that your eyes will be opened to God's reality in your own life. It is my desire that this book will not only be a beacon of hope and comfort to you but that it will make you attentive to the biddings of your Creator for a better connection with Him and a living faith in Christ as your personal Saviour. My prayer is that you shall be rooted and grounded in Him who created and owns all things, especially in these hard days when all many know is doubt and fear. Let Him be the rock that you can anchor your life on!

CHAPTER ONE

Breaking Waters

No good thing will God withhold from them that walk uprightly.

Psalm 84:11

Ever since the dawn of humanity, men and women have sacrificed much to show love. But in my opinion, a woman has especially had much to give for love, particularly when it comes to childbearing. Through the long months of pregnancy, she looks forward to finally meeting that new life – and when the bundle of joy she has been eagerly anticipating arrives, she then showers it with even more tender love and care. For her, it is absolute love for the other; it is all about giving her all. There is no selfishness there.

Consider the pain of labour. It is hard to describe how I felt watching my wife wailing, bashing the car door vigorously and calling on her mother for help, as she frantically battled in vain against the excruciating labour pains tormenting her body. It had become a battle of pain versus love and sacrifice. My wife had reached a point of no return; our baby was on her way out, and that was final. There was no retreating – not that day! Mother nature had no mercy for her, not this time around. The delivery had to proceed. She had to go through it

Breaking Waters

on her own, and she had to win the battle for the sake of her unborn child.

I longed to rub her hand, encourage and assure her, "Oh, my dear! By any means, hang on; everything is going to be OK." But I couldn't rescue or even soothe her as we drove. Fear and nervousness gripped me. In fact, a cocktail of emotions threatened to engulf me. My worst fear was for her to deliver the baby before we could reach the hospital. I could not imagine how we would handle the situation since it was just the two of us on the highway, and to make matters worse, we were both inexperienced and in a state of panic. I kept on praying that we would arrive at the hospital safely. A dream I had had ten months earlier had brought us to this point. Unbelievable!

The more she screamed, the harder I pushed the accelerator. With determination I hit one hundred and eighty kilometres per hour for the first time in my life. I whispered, "Thank you, God, that it's a weekend!" The usually jammed highway had virtually no cars besides us, save for one or two vehicles. It was as if the authorities had commanded them to park and grant us thoroughfare.

As I drove, I started recalling how we had woken up early that Saturday morning with one agenda in mind for that day. The previous day had been my payday and so instead of going to church that morning (may God forgive us!) we had decided to do our final shopping in preparation for the baby's arrival, since we were still unprepared. Even though according to the physician we had two weeks left to the estimated date of delivery, it felt prudent for us to prepare in case of an unexpected early arrival – and the unexpected happened that very day.

We had hardly begun our shopping when my wife started complaining of pain. She did not realize she was experiencing the initial stage of labour. She decided to return to the car, leaving me to carry on with the purchases.

After payment, I hurried back, unaware of how drastically the situation had changed with my wife and how the day's events had taken a different trajectory from what we had planned – very unexpectedly so! I now believe, such is life! Life is packed with such deviations that test us to the limits of our strength. We need to always brace ourselves so we are ready when they happen.

When I got to the car, I was greeted with, "My waters have broken!" The alarm in her voice derailed me, and immediately adrenaline kicked in. I got into the car without wasting any more time.

We had to rush home to get some things for my wife before we could race to the hospital. Even though she was in pain, to try and save time she busied herself as we drove home, selecting the baby's things she would require at the hospital.

Our first child had been born by a prearranged C-section, carried out before my wife went into labour, and so this was our first experience of rushing to the hospital in labour. Panic gripped us because we did not know how much time we had on our side and because it was a thirty-minute drive to the hospital during regular traffic.

It is incredible how our heavenly Father has a thousand ways to provide for us that we are unaware of and a plenitude of ways to eliminate every obstacle we encounter in this world. Amid the burden of the day, there was a divine provision, and we were grateful. Despite our circumstances, I knew it was no surprise to God for my wife to go into labour that day. That is often the case in many situations. There is always something that causes us to thank the Lord. Every day we are surrounded with many tokens of God's love but we often overlook these blessings and instead choose to dwell upon the difficulties of this life. Some, like me in the past, are continually fearful and therefore blinded to the provisions of God. Sadly, we can stumble on these difficulties rather than allowing our problems to draw us to God, as He intends them to. He is our only source of help.

In our case, we had to thank the Lord because my uncle's wife was visiting, and she wasn't planning to leave until the following day, so at least for that day we had someone to stay with our son while we rushed to the hospital. For days before, we had worn ourselves out with continual worry as we had tried to figure out whom to leave our son with when that day would finally come. Now all the worrying and stressing was shown to be needless.

Looking back, I can see how I often caught myself trying too hard to take care of myself while worrying excessively. However, all that effort usually amounted to nothing. I usually struggled with things out of my reach or sphere of influence as if I could gain control of the situation by worrying. After having gone through a lot of 'kicking against the goads' it finally dawned upon me that my excessive worry and uneasiness only testified to my lack of total surrender and dependence upon our heavenly Father, and my inefficiency and weakness without His unique wisdom and grace. We often worry, fear and doubt because we work too much in our strength and lack a firm trust in God. It is only in God that we can prosper. I have learned that in humility and holiness of mind, we will find great peace and strength.

Blessed Assurance

The problem with worry is it is blind and cannot discern the future, but Jesus sees the end from the beginning. In every difficulty, He has a way prepared to bring relief to those who trust and obey Him.

We often mistake worrying for thinking, but the two are different. Worry is going in circles with feelings of anxiety or trouble over an actual or potential problem, and we usually do it without noticing. This repeated process does not yield any positive results or eliminate the real or imagined difficulty, because it is not constructive but destructive. All it does is exacerbate the situation. Worry often puts us in great danger of manufacturing yokes for our necks and makes them more severe and more solemn. We need to do all we can without worrying because worry does not help the matter, but trusting in Christ does.

On the other hand, thinking is purposeful, constructive, organized and a progressive process that we use to make sense of our world. God designed us to think, and He even bids us, "Come now, and let us reason together" (Isaiah 1:18). Correct thinking leads to solutions and, more importantly, the realization that our hope lies in Christ; that realization must drive us to reach out to Him for help.

In our case, we had tired ourselves out with worry, when in fact Jesus had the answer ready for us all along. If we had silenced our hearts in prayer and waited on God, we would have been able to receive his peace. Sometimes in that place of peace, the Holy Spirit leads us to take action. Sometimes we are able to better evaluate the situation. Still other times, we simply have to trust him.

It can sometimes seem difficult or impractical to obey the Word of God by not worrying about the future, especially in the darkest days, when appearances seem most forbidding, but it is in those days that we most need to have faith in God. He has a way of working out His will during those times, doing all things well on behalf of His children.

You may have genuine concerns and burdens to bear in your life that make worry seem irresistible and logical, but I promise you there is much joy and freedom in trusting the Lord your helper always and being about your business for the day. You will also discover your burden becomes lighter and easier to bear, and you will have more time to yourself for other meaningful things in life, such as Bible study and prayer.

Helpful Nuggets

1. Worry is blind and cannot see the future, but Jesus sees the end from the beginning.
2. Correct thinking leads to solutions and, more importantly, the realization that our hope lies in Christ; that realization must drive us to reach out to Him for help.
3. As you trust in the Lord, you will find your burden becomes lighter and easier to bear.

Chapter Two

Blessed Assurance

Before I formed thee in the belly I knew thee; and before thou camest forth out of the womb I sanctified thee, and I ordained thee a prophet unto the nations.

Jeremiah 1:5

Ten months before that day when we drove frantically to the hospital, I had a dream. In my dream I was walking down a narrow, tranquil path. There was no one else there besides me. I started wondering how I got there and could not even work out where it was I was going on that lonely path; it didn't seem to lead anywhere I knew of.

As I perused the surroundings, it appeared others had travelled here before, since there was virtually no grass on the path save for some which bordered its edges. Further down to my left, there was what looked like a plantation of water berry trees. These are medium-sized, evergreen trees with dense, spreading crowns. They usually grow along riverbanks. On the right side, there was a vast open area. As I continued walking along the path, I noticed on the far right a dilapidated table for vendors, which looked like it was abandoned, or maybe it was just too late in the day for anyone to be selling.

Blessed Assurance

Suddenly, I glimpsed a swift movement behind the table, and I realized that I was not alone anymore. I checked closely and noticed a man squatting there as if hiding. He was dressed in white and had long braided hair to disguise himself, but I felt like I recognized him.

He looked up in astonishment but with a twinkle in his eyes because I had managed to locate him despite him being concealed behind the table. He exclaimed with a note of amusement, "You noticed me. I thought no one would find me here." And I nodded in agreement. Then, unexpectedly, the man tossed a small stone in my direction. His abrupt action elicited my reflexive response, and I caught the rock in my hands. Then he rapidly launched another and yet another, all of which I caught. I amazed myself at my swiftness and readiness. The man was impressed, and pleased by my show of dexterity, he began to utter words of blessings over my life, saying, "Because you have successfully captured the stones which I threw at you, now you are not going to lack anything or lose anything in your life."

"Ha! What *blessed assurance*!" My heart was elated upon receiving the blessings. Who could have imagined this could occur on a seemingly lonely path? Certainly not me. I felt a wave of assuredness and comfort all over my body. What was particularly exhilarating and marvellous about the blessings was that they were given to me without me searching for them – by grace.

There had been a few times previous to this that I'd felt the same assuredness. While growing up, my siblings would either tease me or silence me whenever we fought. To put me in my place, they would remind me how they had wanted to flush me down the toilet the day I was born and my mother had to prevent them from fulfilling their evil plan. This mother's love continued to provide a place of refuge and reassurance whenever I was at loggerheads with my siblings. My mother's sweet, consoling and comforting words always soothed me, reassured me and gave me hope and a place in the family. Every child has a fundamental need to feel this assurance of their parents' love and to know they belong.

It was this sense of belonging that my siblings always sought to destabilize. The verbal abuse that made me withdraw later led to rebellion against them, especially when I developed some internal buffers or shock absorbers to make me better able to withstand and resist their attacks. This was a mistake, because I thought I could now fight my own battles and rarely went to my mother for comfort like I used to. It was also a mistake because I met with more torment than before. Sometimes things got physical and, being young, I was always at the receiving end of brutal and merciless blows.

Isn't this familiar? This is what we usually do when faced with difficult situations, especially relational ones. We become bitter and overburdened with life because we stop seeking refuge in the Lord's arms, just like as a child I should have sought refuge in my mother. We prefer to handle our affairs alone, but we receive more bodily and emotional harm this way. Afterward, battered and bruised, some realize it does not have to be this way; there is help available. Others do not even realize their helplessness and need for assistance until it is too late. But for those who seek the Lord, it will never be too late. He is there, longing for you to ask Him for help.

My siblings had threatened to flush me away because I was born a male child when they were all expecting a female, based on their assumption that I would follow the alternating girl →

boy → girl → boy pattern in our family. The fourth child in the family was a boy and so it made sense that the fifth would be a girl – but *boom!* To everyone's dismay I disrupted the pattern. My presence disturbed my siblings' emotions to the extent that they wanted to flush me away.

I never entirely blamed them for feeling that way. It is human nature to want things to follow a specific pattern or tradition, society's norm, and those who deviate are usually met with resistance and ruthlessness. Some like things to stay predictably the way they are. Consider Jesus, for example. The Pharisees and Sadducees fought Him. They saw Jesus as a threat because He challenged their traditions, which they held so dearly even to the point of orchestrating the crucifixion of the only begotten Son of God. We can also consider Saul before he became Paul. He was on a rampage murdering Christians because he thought they were blasphemous. Even on the day he encountered Jesus Christ on the road to Damascus, he was on a mission to murder Christians.

However, it is a fallacy in this imperfect and ever-changing world to expect things to remain predictable and within our control. This ingrained desire for predictability traps many people in apprehensiveness and worry, because uncertainty in this world is inevitable. It is better to keep an open mind, knowing that we do not know everything and not everything is in our control. When the unforeseen happens, as it inevitably does, we need to be flexible enough to adjust and adapt to the new norm.

God gave me reassurance later in my life when I read the verse at the start of this chapter, Jeremiah 1:5. It penetrated my being right through to my marrow, and it still does to this day. It changed my worldview forever. I used to think I disrupted the norm in the family – but no, it was not of my doing. God influenced everything. Heaven wanted me; God had to interrupt the tradition that had been set in my family for a reason. My siblings and my parents were expecting a female child, but God had something else packaged for them for a purpose.

Sometimes the things we hold dear and are willing to defend in this life are frivolous when weighed against God's standard and His plans for our lives and nations at large. He sees the big picture of things. His thoughts are not like our little thoughts. We think primarily of ourselves and our immediate circumstances. But it is a mistake to insist on clinging to our ideals when God is pointing in another direction. Like Jeremiah, we are all ordained for a particular purpose in this world. We must seek Him and His Kingdom first, as Jesus admonished in Matthew 6:33: "But seek ye first the kingdom of God, and his righteousness; and all these things shall be added unto you."

In my dream, I resumed down the path, feeling satisfied as I meditated upon what had just transpired. I kept repeating the sweet words that I would not lack anything or lose anything in my life.

Considering my circumstances at the time, the proclamation was puzzling. Still in the dream, I was thinking about the meaning of the stones: "Could they be representing my family?" I thought to myself – the three stones representing my son, my wife and me?

If it meant my family, the reassurance was welcome; I had a deep-seated fear at that time of losing loved ones. No one wants to lose their loved ones even though it is a fact of life that none of us are going to be here forever. One way or another, we will lose those dear to us at some point. Even so, the reassurance created a sense of contentment within me.

Still engrossed in my thoughts, in my dream, I reached yet another open ground that looked like a soccer pitch. There were people engaged in praise and worship. I was so intrigued by their melodious singing and dancing that I stood there marvelling at what was taking place.

Then a woman came out of the congregation and started to walk toward me. Suddenly, I found myself lying on the ground and the woman started speaking. It seemed like she was prophesying over my life again. She said, "You are going to have a child. The child will be chosen, precious and special."

This was good news, I was enthused by the thought of having another child even though we had not planned to have one, but something was flummoxing about what she said. It bothered me that she used the words "precious" and "special" in the same sentence. I was OK with "precious" but not "special". My mind immediately rushed to what I dreaded the most then; maybe it meant the child would have special needs and would require extraordinary care. It troubled my mind and led me to question the dream. Were the people I had met really messengers of God or was the dream just a consequence of the food I had eaten that night?

I woke up still trying to figure out the dream, and I told my wife about those I had perceived to be heavenly messengers and the message they had brought us. I also told her of my great concern, the "specialness" of the baby. She shared the same sentiments. That I questioned the dream based on the negative connotation I had attached to the word "special" only revealed my deep-seated fear and prejudice against having a child with special needs. As someone who desires to be Christlike in character, this attitude had to be uprooted. We had to move from a state of conditional love and rejection to a state of unconditional love and acceptance.

Deciding what to do from a position of fear and worry is usually tricky, if not paralyzing; there are always the 'what ifs'. We are driven to focus intently on the problems that may occur if we were to take one particular course or the other, forgetting that we will never know the outcome, whether good or bad, until we decide to act regardless. If things turn out to be wrong, we usually quickly find a better way around the problem in reality than we are able to in our imagination, for we always imagine the worst from a position of fear and worry.

In our case, however, we reached an agreement to have the baby no matter how it would be. If the child was from God, it was our gift. We have blessed assurance in God, who knows all things. John says:

> *Our actions will show that we belong to the truth, so we will be confident when we stand before God ... Those who obey God's commandments remain in fellowship with him, and he with them. And we know he lives in us because the Spirit he gave us lives in us.*
>
> 1 John 3:19-24 (NLT)

Whenever I reach moments like these when I doubt or question if I am really hearing from God, the Holy Spirit is quick to jog my mind into remembering the incredible work God has been, and is, doing in my life. I find my assurance in what God has done in my life thus far. I also gather confidence whenever I align my actions with the Word of God. Whenever I live in obedience to His commandments, things work together for good for me. I enjoy the fruits of fellowshipping with Him and having my assurance in Him. We abide in the Lord because of who He is and the work He seeks to accomplish in us. Whenever I look back in hindsight, the dots connect perfectly. The Holy Spirit is referred to as another Comforter by Jesus, and I can see His work in my life. He has been my very present teacher and source of comfort.

Having fellowship with Him before and looking at how He had reached for me, I was confident the dream was from Him despite all that perturbed me.

Helpful Nuggets

1. We prefer to handle our affairs alone, but the Lord is longing for you to ask Him for help.
2. You are here because heaven wanted you!
3. We can find assurance in what God has done in our life so far.

Chapter Three

Pregnancy and the Awaited News

Faith is the substance of things hoped for, the evidence of things not seen.

Hebrews 11:1

Within a few weeks from the day that I had the dream promising us a child, my wife got pregnant. We had decided to take a leap of faith despite our worst fears. We had concluded that whatever happened would be God's will for us, and we only needed to submit our will to His, because He always has our best interest in mind even when we do not comprehend it. Besides, our love for Him constrains us to do His will, and by choosing to abide by it, we were demonstrating our love and faith in Him.

Truth is defined by God, not by me or someone else. Faith, then, means making God's reality the foundation or support of our actions, giving us a positive outlook. This faith does not originate with people but with God Himself and can only be imparted to us through hearing His Word ("So then faith cometh by hearing, and hearing by the word of God" – Romans 10:17).

This means that the more we expose ourselves to God's Word and the more we delve into scriptures through the study of the Bible, spiritual material and listening to sermons, the

Pregnancy and the Awaited News

more we gain greater clarity and understanding of God and His governance as He reveals Himself to us. The process by which He shows Himself to us awakens in us a desire to put our trust in Him, knowing that He will not fail us as He is the Almighty God whose ways are different from ours and who has our best interests at heart, anchored on His love for us.

The Bible says that faith as little as a mustard seed has enough power to uproot a mountain or colossal obstacle and throw it into the sea. In our case, the mountain was not the condition of the baby. The colossal block that had to be thrown into the sea was our lack of unconditional love. At the time, we were not willing to have a baby that had special needs. That was entirely outside of what we had imagined and were prepared to manage as a young couple. Even while living in a world marred by sin and its consequences, we still expected to have a wonderful and perfect family like any other couple we could think of.

It was not until we decided to function from God's reality that the mountain was uprooted from deep down our hearts and was cast off into the sea, that we immediately found peace within our hearts to accept whatever eventuality we would face soon.

Soon we found ourselves eighteen weeks into the pregnancy, and we decided it was time to register with an obstetrician.

When we arrived at the practice, I was a bit apprehensive because it was now time to confirm the reality. Would our child have special needs? Even though we had resolved to accept any outcome, reconciling that decision now with the actual reality made me nervous and uncertain that I could bear the news well.

We had brought our son along to the appointment; at that time, he was a naughty three-year-old. I was soon recruited to be the childminder while we waited for our turn. He ran around and played with the water dispenser. Usually this behaviour would not be tolerated and would receive the proper correction, but it was a welcome distraction under the circumstances. Chasing after him and restraining him kept me distracted from my depressing fears, and soon we were called in to see the specialist.

We were greeted with a warm and inviting smile from the physician. He was tall and slim, with a dark complexion. He gestured us to take our seats.

I took a quick glance around the office; it was nicely arrayed with machines that appeared advanced. Then I was interrupted by a calm and deep voice as the physician asked how he could assist us, and my wife briefed him on the purpose of our visit.

She was asked to go and lie on the bed for a scan. The procedure went smoothly, and the physician even asked us if we were willing to know the gender of the baby, to which I exclaimed, "Yes, sir!" He checked and informed us that we were going to have a baby girl.

I had always wanted a baby girl, which I think might just be every father's wish. But I was a bit perplexed, because from the dream I had concluded the child was going to be a boy, given the nature of the profession I had presumed for the child. I thought the child was going to be a pastor or a minister of the gospel.

The doctor explained the results he had obtained from his measurements and other vital checks. He said, "I didn't see anything wrong with the foetus; everything looks normal to me, but unfortunately, it's already too late to check for Down syndrome. You were supposed to come earlier for us to be able to do that test."

He explained why some tests were conducted at an earlier stage and then he told us there was no need to come back for another review soon, as he usually only required that when he suspected problems. Instead we were asked to come back at twenty-six weeks for the growth scan. He also stressed that if my wife felt discomfort, however slight, she should come without waiting for the next appointment date.

A wave of relief burst from our lungs into the air, leaving us at ease and with our anxiety and fears abated. Now we were more determined to have this baby. We were so thankful and happy to be expecting and to have taken that leap of faith.

And so, we went home with uplifted moods; we felt much better and taller than when we had walked into the practice. Our conversations were more positive; we discussed names for the baby and what we wanted to buy for her. We decided this time my wife would choose the baby's first name since I had decided for our son last time.

We started comparing names until we settled on Avery, meaning 'counsellor', and for her second name we chose Tawana, which is a Shona name meaning 'we have' in English.

Our baby was growing fast; my wife could feel her movements and kicks in her womb. There were ecstatic and heart-warming moments when I too felt her kicking. What a wonderful feeling!

Now fear, they say, is False Evidence Appearing Real. When we are afraid we are basing our feelings on something that is not actually there, on something that is imagined, until it seems real and is terrifying to us. We experience the terror before the thing we fear actually happens. Fear is simply a signal that I have shifted my focus and trust from God and on to myself to bear any given situation. Thinking about this made me remember how the apostle Peter got out of the boat to join Jesus, who was walking on water. For the time Peter's eyes remained transfixed on Jesus, he was able to walk on water. Not until the moment he shifted his eyes from the Master did he begin to sink. So, without the signal of fear, we would never know when we have drifted away from His presence. Relying on myself and not the omniscient One would be a passport to fear.

No matter how robust or capable we are, there are so many things that fail us as human beings. There are elements beyond our reach that can derail our plans or interfere with our intentions, such as natural disasters or accidents on the highway caused by mechanical failure. Fear constrains you; it immobilizes you and imprisons you somehow, subconsciously telling you there must never be a time that you go out there on your own. But faith is the opposite of fear. Faith shifts your focus and trust from yourself and on to God. Faith liberates; it empowers you and leads you to action. It leads you to deal easily with any situation which you would otherwise deem unthinkable and impossible, because the omniscient One is enabling you.

Helpful Nuggets

1. Faith means making God's reality the foundation or support of our actions, giving us a positive outlook.
2. God has our best interests at heart.

3. Fear is a signal that we have shifted our focus and trust from God to ourselves in any given situation. Without that signal, we would never know when we would have drifted away from His presence.

Chapter Four

A Test of Faith

Faith is the substance of things hoped for, the evidence of things not seen.

Hebrews 11:1

Sooner than we knew, it was already time for our second visit to the doctor. It was now twenty-six weeks into the pregnancy. When we got to the practice, the waiting room was packed. We quickly joined the queue. This time around, we were relaxed as we felt we had nothing to fear. We were comfortable and sure of our situation.

I started looking around; I noticed most ladies came alone for the routine checks as there were only one or two other dads accompanying their spouses for the regular check-up. I caught myself judging the absent men, wondering where they were and how they could let their wives go through this experience alone; then I quickly reminded myself that circumstances sometimes don't allow us to be physically present when it matters the most for our spouses and the unborn babies.

I remembered how it happened to me with our first child. My wife and I were thousands of miles apart throughout the gestation period. I was working in another continent while my wife was back home, where she was also working. While still absorbed in my thoughts, it was our turn again.

A Test of Faith

We were greeted with the same warm and welcoming smile, and we were gestured again to take our seats. My wife sat on the bed, and my son and I sat on the chair. Without delay, the physician began the scan with an expressionless face. After a while, his face adopted a strange expression as he repeatedly took measurements of the baby's brain and kept on mapping the heart with the knob of the scanner. I could sense the tightening in his body, and his growing concern was contagious. I felt my initial enthusiasm ebbing out of me. No one spoke, and it seemed like we were heading for eternity; agitation and apprehension gripped me tighter with every passing moment. I wondered if it was just my imagination beguiling me or whether there really was something very wrong.

Eventually, he broke the silence with a soft, careful and gloomy tone. He informed us that something was wrong with the baby's brain – there was an abnormal gap for the cerebrospinal fluid, and the heart appeared like it had a hole. He recommended a second opinion before saying something conclusive, but he suspected a chromosomal defect. He did not specify which one.

It felt like a heavy concrete block was released from the skies and it fell straight on my head, crushing me down to the ground, where I was only to be greeted by the hard floor, sandwiching me between the two.

A solemn atmosphere pervaded the room while our hopes and excitement instantly drained out of our systems and in their place squatted despondency and melancholy.

The physician made an appointment for us with a specialist colleague of his. According to him, she was better positioned to accurately identify what was happening, due to her more advanced equipment which could produce coloured scans. We were scheduled to go the following week.

We left the room feeling as if we were covered by a heavy and very dark cloud. Neither of us uttered a word as we individually brooded over the information, struggling to contain or understand what had just transpired.

"What could have gone wrong?" I pondered to myself. "Wasn't everything fine the last time we were there?" Where was this all coming from? What was happening to our lovely and promising girl? She had had a healthy future ahead of her. Why this now, and especially why *her?* My thoughts continued and questions raced through my head.

My wife and I have the same temperament; we tend to get absorbed in ourselves while processing information. At times like these, we crave to be alone for a while before talking to anyone. When we were still courting, one of my friends teased me, wondering how we communicated and who usually started the conversations since we were both notorious for being incredibly quiet.

We only discussed the news that had pierced and rippled through both our hearts like a dagger when we got home. We couldn't understand what had occurred since our previous visit. "Everything is normal," the doctor had stated back then. How I wished I could hear him repeat the same words, reassuring us that everything was perfect.

"Could it be Down syndrome?" I inquired. Being a registered nurse, I thought my wife would know.

"No, I do not think so; Down syndrome usually does not exhibit those symptoms; it could be something else. Let us wait for the specialist next week rather than speculating now," she replied, cautioning me.

A Test of Faith

I remembered the dream. "Maybe this is what was meant in my dream. Maybe we were being warned of what the devil was brewing for us."

"Yeah, maybe," she agreed expressionlessly.

"Since I think we were warned for a reason, let us pray for God to fix this situation on our behalf. I also think something of this nature requires us to fast. However, since you are pregnant, just engage yourself in prayers while I do both. I will fast until delivery," I suggested assuredly.

"True. Let's do that," she agreed again, and then she started playing with our son to divert her attention from the depressing thoughts.

I reached for my mobile phone and started Googling about congenital chromosomal abnormalities. I later found out that trisomy 13 matched what the doctor had described, and that the prognosis was abysmal. I discovered that the two most severe congenital defects are trisomy 13 and trisomy 18. Children with such defects died young.

I was more broken than ever. I refused for my daughter to have any of those defects. I became more determined to fast and pray. Not that I was the fasting type. Before this, I rarely fasted, as I could not resist the temptation of food, but this time I had to. Who would not for their child? My love for her compelled me. A father's love! There had to be a miraculous intervention from above.

Now, this was an actual test of faith.

Monday arrived, the day for us to visit the specialist. She was based at a private hospital in Pretoria, about thirty minutes' drive from where we lived.

The physician looked young, about my own age. She greeted us courteously and gestured us to take our seats. After we briefed her on the purpose of our visit, she instructed my wife to lie on the bed so that she could examine the pregnancy.

She discovered that our daughter had hypoplastic left heart syndrome, extra digits, and it also appeared that she had club feet. These congenital abnormalities are often found in children with trisomy 13. According to her, that is what our child had. We were then asked to consult with a paediatric cardiologist to further investigate the baby's heart condition. She made the first appointment for us and booked it for the Wednesday of that week.

Even though we had seen it coming, it was hard for us to endure the news. It was now confirmed; our worst fears had been realized. A plethora of thoughts flooded my mind once more. I had so many questions, wondering what more lay ahead of us. Were we ready for this journey? But our baby was said to be precious and chosen; how was that possible when the prognosis was poor? Why had I heard in my dream that I would not lose anything in my life? "Lord, what is happening?" I prayed. "I need you now; I need answers!"

The news had the potential of shattering my hopes completely, but a still, small voice reached me. It kept referring me back to the dream, despite the dark cloud enveloping me. Thank God I could still hear that soft whisper, and that it was enough to stop me from shattering altogether.

It does not matter what situation you find yourself in, there is always that tiny window of hope; there is always that ray of light that penetrates the darkest of clouds to shine upon your heart. It is up to you whether you focus on the vast cloud threatening to engulf you or whether you hold on to that tiny glimmer of light; it is enough to make a deep impact on your heart. Press on with all your strength, because your life depends upon it.

In any given situation, you must exercise your free will. You will always be presented with what feels like an insurmountable problem and also the brightest glimmer of hope. It is up to you to keep this hope alive by feeding it until it overpowers the darkness in you. It feels so tiny but it is all you need. There is a bolt of power in that little flicker. It demonstrates the ability of light over darkness, but it only is effective in those who are willing, unlike the darkness that just bulldozes through.

I am glad I chose the glimmer and fed it by focusing on the Word and on my dream. For "the just shall live by his faith" (Hab.2:4)! We were going to have the baby, full stop!

Helpful Nuggets

1. God often speaks with a still, small voice; we need to pay attention when He does!
2. No matter what situation you find yourself in, there is always a tiny window of hope.
3. When God gives hope, it is up to us to keep it alive by feeding it.

Chapter Five

Learning to Trust God

Trust in the Lord with all thine heart; and lean not unto thine own understanding.

Proverbs 3:5

Faith is something that God grows within us gradually as believers. There is a step of faith when we are born again, but we also need to receive faith for the trials that we face. In this chapter I will tell a story from earlier in my life, which shows how God began to teach me to trust him, preparing the way for the events that would follow later.

It all started with a dream. I found myself moving quickly, engrossed by terror and nervous apprehension as I descended a long, shadowy tunnel while being pursued by what I perceived to be an extremely hungry and very large creature. I could almost feel its tentacles on my back as it snarled at me, with the reverberations of its stomping and the sound of its clangour further exacerbating the dire situation. I became terrified as the grisly thought of being turned into a meal began to take on more reality. Refusing to become dinner, I ran as hard as I could to escape from the tunnel with my life. As I fled, I saw that up ahead the tunnel divided into two, and at that juncture indecision bludgeoned me. "Shall I turn to the right or to the left?" I despaired. But just as I reached the divergence, a sharp voice pierced through both the thundering noises in the tunnel and my confusion. I was not alone in the tunnel with the hideous creature after all! I heard a clear and precise instruction to manoeuvre to the right. I instinctively followed the directive. I barely dodged the monster's jaws and bolted away even as the sun's rays began to appear, signalling that I was now on the verge of arriving at the other end of the tunnel. This only fuelled and ignited more energy; I felt a surge of new power travel through my muscles propelling me along as a strong realization dawned upon me that there was still hope of seeing the sunshine again. Not until I reached daylight did I cease running. A sigh of victory escaped my lungs, and I began waving my hands in the air as if doing a victory dance. The win was mine; the creature's desire to transform me into dinner had failed and was not going to be fulfilled any time soon. How exceedingly joyous and indeed thankful I was to have survived such a harrowing ordeal, relatively unscathed save for the emotional trauma of this horror-movie-like experience!

As I reflected upon the dream, it struck me that perhaps something drastic was about to take place in the next phase of my life. And when that time came, I had to listen to and follow someone else's advice to avoid making the wrong decision, just as I'd had to in my dream.

This dream occurred on the eve of my second year of college and just before we had to choose our trades. The first year had consisted of basic training in general aircraft maintenance. During that time, students familiarized themselves with different trades available so that when the time to specialize in the second year, we would know what to choose.

At that time, sheet metal work appealed to me, and it was in demand in various countries abroad, so I had determined to specialize in it.

The following morning at the technical school, we were exhilarated, as well as slightly tense, because this day would affect our careers forever if we chose to stay in the aviation industry. We were in groups discussing for the final time what we were going to choose and why we thought that trade was lucrative.

Then the moment we were anticipating finally arrived as the manager walked in; we promptly took our seats in respect of the big man. He instantly began calling out the various trades. Those interested in each discipline were instructed to compile a list of their names. The manager required only six people for training in sheet metal, but seven of us were interested in it. He asked one of us to volunteer for a different craft, but no one would budge on their choice. We all wanted sheet metal and were not willing to take any option that we would regret in the future. Without wasting much of his time, he left for his office, leaving us to discuss and decide who would be the sacrificial lamb.

We remained in limbo, weighing up the options and trying to figure out the next best choice. That is when it hit me: "Don't listen to yourself but someone else." I have come to think that it was the Holy Spirit who prompted me to remember the dream and bid me to follow the instruction. Straightaway I got out of my chair and followed the manager to his office.

By now, I was wiser and knew better to follow instructions of this nature from my dreams. On a previous occasion when I believe God's messenger visited me in my sleep, I ignored the

Learning to Trust God

vision and did nothing with the message. It ended up tragically. From that time, I chose to take notice whenever I had a vivid dream that woke me up filled with emotions, either good or bad, and that lingered on during my waking hours. I also noticed that these dreams occurred whenever something was about to happen that could alter my life in an upward or downward trajectory.

The dreams with an upward trajectory led me to celebrate in Christ even before the things came to pass, and they also helped my faith in God. Those with a downward trajectory led me to pray to God in the hope He would relent and prevent the event from occurring, but if He did not, they were still a source of comfort. The warnings always alerted and comforted me beforehand and dampened the impact of the actual event. The signs only confirmed the words of Jesus that He was going to leave us with another Comforter.

As soon as I arrived at the manager's office, I expressed my willingness to volunteer and asked him which trade he would recommend for me to choose.

His stern expression unwound into an approving smile. "You have made the right decision," he chuckled, and he went on to reveal that there was another new trade called aircraft composites. I was surprised, because we had never heard of it during the past year and only now was he mentioning it. There was only one other person who had chosen this trade after consulting with him.

He disclosed that both of us would be the first formal students in that trade at the institution. He saved the best part for last. He revealed that those specialising in composites would also specialise in sheet metal, but not vice versa. Wow, this made my day! Even as I write this many years later, I can almost feel the same elation I had back then. I was so pleased I had obeyed the voice in my dream.

The fact that the advice from the dream was so timely further strengthened my trust in God. I have come to see that with every trial or situation like this, God's purpose is to build rapport with me, increasing my dependency on Him in all situations.

This rapport-building in my private life is to create a solid relationship or connection based on trust between God and me in preparation for my deployment. We get saved to serve others. I need to be standing on solid ground, knowing that He is with me all the way and that He can always come through for me whenever the need arises. When the Lord intends to use you for something big, He first appears to you privately for some rapport-building, strengthening you in Himself. The Lord is reaching out to all of us in different private ways so that we may know Him for who He truly is and that we may find our identity in Him. We all have something to do in this world for Him.

Helpful Nuggets

1. Faith is something that God grows within us gradually.
2. With every trial, God's purpose is to build rapport with us.
3. We get saved to serve others!

Chapter Six

The Cost of Obedience

Let us hold fast the profession of our faith without wavering; (for he is faithful that promised)...
Hebrews 10:23

At the government hospital that we were referred to, the cardiologist did an echocardiogram. The heavy and dark cloud over us seemed malignant. The results showed that our baby had two primary heart conditions: hypoplastic left heart syndrome, that the previous physician had detected, and now also truncus arteriosus. The brain's problem seemed dwarfed by this new discovery as the doctors were now mainly focusing on the heart condition.

In layman's terms, the baby's left ventricle of the heart had not developed at all. That is why our initial physician thought her heart had a hole. And the second problem was that the aorta, the blood vessel that would normally come out of the left ventricle, also hadn't developed.

They explained that they wouldn't be able to perform any operation on the heart because of the combination of the two conditions. In the eventuality that the baby miraculously survived, she would not be able to do anything due to the strain on her heart plus a lack of oxygen in the body. Thus, the physicians explained, there would be an incredible toll on us as parents, as well as on our other child since he would not be able to understand why he couldn't play with his sister.

After weighing the situation, they suggested we terminate the pregnancy to redeem the situation. However, the decision was for us to make, as well as in consultation with the baby's grandparents. They gave us one week to mull over our choices – whether termination or continuance of the pregnancy.

They gave us a document with a detailed explanation of the diseases to help with the decision-making process. Could it get any worse than this? Personally, I think no parent should ever be asked to murder their child regardless of how dire the situation may appear to be. It is simply unthinkable and repulsive. We are meant to procreate, cherish, care and protect our little ones. We are not murderers; we are not monsters; we are parents. Honestly, how could I terminate my little girl's life? It jolted me back to the feelings of despair and rejection I had experienced in childhood whenever my siblings had wielded that reminder that they wanted to flush me away when they discovered that I was a boy. Now it was my little girl – and to make matters worse, the one who had once been rejected was now the one being asked to reject. How unpredictably the wheels of life turn... I never thought it would be me who would be asked to consider taking my own child's life in order to abate society's dread of pain and inconvenience.

My innocent little girl was facing the call to be rejected and terminated in order to save her from suffering and us from the inconvenience and burden that her life would bring into our lives. We were told she would tie us down and drain us to exhaustion, giving us a life that was in contradiction with society's values today. Nowadays, communities give greater

The Cost of Obedience

weight to a materialistic lifestyle, a life valuing self-centeredness and convenience over the virtues of self-sacrifice and pledging allegiance to the Creator regardless of the situation. The child had no say in being born. And now, without her consent or chance at life, she was at risk of being sent back again.

Oh God, where are you when all of this is happening? What about your promise that I will not lose anything in life? Was the dream really from you, or have I succumbed to one of the devil's wiles? If it was from you, how can you overlook this tragedy? Has it escaped your watchful eyes? Or do you want us to murder our child?

As these thoughts swept over me, tears filled my eyes. I could feel a lightness in my stomach. Fear, nausea and regret filled every part of my body; it was an awful sensation.

I was there! Utterly where the devil wanted me to be. He had succeeded in trapping me in a corner, a place where I might doubt God and question His presence and love in my life. This is indeed what the devil wants us to do at any given moment or situation: to doubt, and question His presence in our lives and His love for us. The devil wishes us to ask, "If He loves us, why would He allow tragedy to befall us, especially in this way?" The devil's intention is for us to abandon our worship of God and label Him unjust. This is the false accusation he has made against God ever since he revolted against Him in heaven.

Then I remembered Jesus, our Redeemer in Gethsemane. (Make the Bible your companion! It is the best tool for reassurance, comfort and hope whenever you seek clarity for any situation you may find yourself in.) Jesus agonized to the point of having sweat-like droplets of blood as He wrestled with doubt. His eternity and position in heaven were in jeopardy. If He proceeded with the plan of our salvation, one mistake could cost Him His life forever. He was risking being separated from His Father forever. Despite knowing the potential consequences, He chose to submit His will to His Father's will. That is lived obedience; that is self-sacrifice for others; that is humility; above all, that is love! Satan's dismal attempt to sow doubt in Him and sabotage the plan of salvation decided upon even before the foundation of the world had been stopped. Furthermore, despite His foreknowledge, God created us all, both die-hard sinners and those who would repent. He gave us all a chance at life. Even those that were going to join His archrival were still given an opportunity.

Being a partaker of His tremendous mercy, how could I succumb to the doctor's well-meaning but brutal suggestion to terminate the life of not only my lovely daughter but another creation of God, based on the poor prognosis?

I unequivocally determined to shame the devil by engaging in the situation with faith rather than fear. I was faced with two realities: the reality the physicians presented; and the other spiritual reality revealed in the dream. The first reality I could relate to and understand easily; I could wrap my mind around it because it was taking place in my realm, as opposed to the other reality based on the sole belief that my dream was from God. Well, I chose to cling to the reality I believed was *God's* reality, despite my lack of understanding of how things were going to unfold and despite the temptation from the devil to doubt if it really was God's will I was following.

Proverbs 3:5 instructs, "Trust in the Lord with all thine heart and lean not unto thine own understanding." I tailored my actions in accordance with this instruction. I have discovered that without God, the things we fear most can come to pass and cause deep emotional distress. However, when we trust in God, we may imagine His plans for our lives to be intensely undesirable, yet they turn out to be the most gratifying experiences that could ever happen to us. His plans lead to everlasting life.

The amount of violence against women and children in this world testifies how, as men, we have failed to remain nailed to the cross with Christ. If self remains on the throne of our hearts instead of Jesus, we will never have true peace in the home – or ultimately in the world. The devil will continue with his voracious and ruthless attacks on the family to prevent us from experiencing the true nature of God. Rather than seeking happiness directly in our marriages, let us pursue Christlikeness in those marriages. By seeking to become more like Christ, joy instead will naturally be added unto us. Even if our efforts may not be appreciated, we will still be joyful and have a peace that surpasses all understanding. If only we could realize that!

During our early years of marriage, I once had to make a U-turn from my journey to my parents' home after being convicted by the Holy Spirit. I was like a Jonah on the run or a Saul on the road to Damascus. After an argument during my visit home from Abu Dhabi, where I worked at the time, my wife had lapsed into giving me one of her silent treatments. To get back at her after she left for work, I decided to go to my parents' house without informing her.

On the way, the bus I had boarded developed a problem shortly after departing. To fix the problem, they used a piece of rubber. That did not go down well with the passengers, who started demanding a refund or to be given a different bus. The passengers saw an accident waiting to happen, but the driver and the conductor insisted on proceeding with the journey using the same bus.

When we came to a traffic police roadblock, the people saw an opportunity to report to the police officers their grievances. The traffic police officers instructed the driver to take the bus to the nearest police station to handle the dispute between the driver and the passengers.

While the driver was still negotiating with the police about giving us a refund at the police station, a still, small voice showed up. We had a moment's tête-à-tête. The incident reminded me of a similar incident that occurred in the Bible when Jonah ran away from the presence of God. The storm, in my case, was the problem with the bus. Could it be I was the cause of this problem, or was it just a coincidence? I wondered why I had chosen this bus of all the buses at the rank. I had purposely chosen not to board another bus there because it was notorious for having breakdowns. This one had looked new and reliable enough to take me home without breaking down, but now here we were. Coincidence or not, being a Christian and one who mostly lived by faith and who applied gems from the Bible in his day-to-day living, I decided to get off the bus and go home to face my wife, the one I had chosen to cleave to.

At the time, I still did not quite grasp the concept of a man leaving his parents and cleaving to his wife. I was still focusing on cleaving to my own way of doing things, the way I was accustomed to and had acquired from my previous unexamined experiences. I was unwilling to let go of everything. I was unwilling to choose to build something new

The Cost of Obedience

with my wife. I was unwilling to start afresh and create something that included and accommodated both of our interests.

We were both supposed to be there for one another, banishing selfishness and cleaving to each other. But I had a bone of contention with God: why was I not allowed to have my own selfish way while it seemed she could get away with hers? Why was I not permitted to let her taste some of her own medicine? Oh, why was I denied the pleasure I had imagined I would get when it would have finally dawned on her that I was not coming home? The answer to those selfish questions did not come at that time, but from that day onwards, I realized I was 'kicking against the goads' and would not win in life unless I chose to resolutely commit to building my marriage. Once I made that resolution, I came across a wealth of biblical material that helped me understand the purpose of marriage and the husband's position in the home.

I learned that everything that God has done for people is to enable them to know Him. One of the ways God has desired to disclose Himself to us is through the gift of marriage. Consequently, the purpose of marriage is to reveal the character of God and for us to be acquainted with His nature. He has sought for the Christian family to represent heaven, but only the home where selfless love reigns can do this well. God wants every home on earth to be a symbol of the heavenly abode. In that family setting, the man represents Christ, and he is to love his wife the way Christ loved the church, even to the point of being nailed on to the cross. If the level of sacrifice of the man is to be like Christ nailed to the cross, that means there is no room for revenge, there is no room for hurting his wife and no room for any other form of abuse. Trying to flee in revenge meant that I had broken away from the cross, and in His mercy, God stopped me in my tracks.

I was the first person to leave the scene that day on the bus. I left without knowing or being interested in how it would all end. Everything else became meaningless once I realized I was on the wrong path for my life; not even the hope of a refund could hold me back! I left everything and went home. But – wait a minute! – wasn't the journey to my parents' house leading me home? I realized that now I had a new home. I had left the old one when I agreed to marry my wife and decided to cleave to her only.

The devil can bring disarray into families if he can convince the husband / wife / parents to act in their own interests above the interests of other family members. Now my wife and I were being encouraged to put our own interests above those of our unborn baby – but by God's grace we were able to resist and walk by faith.

Helpful Nuggets

1. No parent should ever be asked to murder their child regardless of how dire the situation may appear to be.
2. True humility and obedience are evidenced in submitting to the Father's will, just as Jesus did.
3. If self remains on the throne of our hearts instead of Christ, we will never have true peace in the home and ultimately in the world.

Chapter Seven

Finding the Holy Spirit's Comfort

Nevertheless, I tell you the truth; it is expedient for you that I go away: for if I go not away, the Comforter will not come unto you; but if I depart, I will send him unto you.

John 16:7

Having chosen to cleave to the promise of God, it struck me that perhaps I had been forewarned in my dream to prepare me for this time. Perhaps the dream was given to enable me to handle the situation appropriately when things unfolded as they had, so that I would know where to turn for help if the situation exceeded my ability to deal with it. Perhaps the dream was given so that I would trust completely in the One who knew beforehand what would happen, and adhere to His way rather than the doctors' way, despite my lack of understanding.

When Jesus was about to go to His Father, He promised to leave His disciples with another Comforter, the Holy Spirit. By calling the Holy Spirit "another Comforter" (John 14:16), Jesus indicates that the Holy Spirit is equal to Him. By referring to the Holy Spirit as a "He", Jesus shows that the Holy Spirit is a person and not, as some well-meaning believers say, an "it". To them, the Holy Spirit is not a person but a force or power they can summon and command as they please. We need to be careful not to see the Holy Spirit as something to manipulate, but rather as someone to comfort, guide, teach, instruct and prompt us to remember whatever we have been taught whenever we are at the crossroads. He is a person who, above all, adorns us with the fruit of the Spirit and spiritual gifts.

I have come to the realization that most of my comfort emanates from the inside. Most of the time when I am in a situation, the people who come to comfort me or to give me counsel only concur with what has already been revealed to me, and at times, they simplify concepts that I have been grappling with. I believe this is because the Holy Spirit is working in all of us, directing and guiding us.

The scans, for example, concurred with the dream I had had before we had ever thought of having another child. The impact of the test results was less devastating than it would have been if I hadn't been forewarned. This is how God has operated in my life.

Before any one of His children gets into a predicament, God is already there; He is never late, He does not deal in afterthoughts and He is never caught off guard. In Daniel 3, for example, we mustn't think God commenced His rescue operation after Shadrach, Meshach and Abednego had been cast into the fire. Long before King Nebuchadnezzar decided to throw the boys in, God had turned the fiery furnace into a spiritual rendezvous point in anticipation of the arrival of the three faithful and unwavering Hebrews. God provided an excellent opportunity to further fortify their belief and faith by demonstrating to the king that not even death, or the threat

Finding the Holy Spirit's Comfort

of it, was enough to stop them worshipping the only true God, the God of the heavens and the earth and everything within them.

The modern technology only served to confirm what had been foretold already in the dream.

> *...God is faithful, who will not suffer you to be tempted above that ye are able; but will with the temptation also make a way to escape, that ye may be able to bear it.*
>
> *1 Corinthians 10:13*

A provision to escape had been provided for me beforehand. Cooperation with the Creator meant I had to cleave to the promise of having a baby.

A while ago, after writing the first draft of this book, I fell sick. I felt pain on the left side of my stomach, which was present for quite some time before I could go to the doctor. When I could not take it anymore, I went to consult with my GP. When I informed her that I had had the pain for a long time, she referred me to a specialist. The specialist could not find anything from the blood sample and scan, and so he decided to perform a laparoscopy on me. I went through the procedure, then the following day after the operation, I began to feel constipated and bloated. It was now a Friday; I called the practice again to book an appointment with the physician because I felt unwell, and I thought it could be because of the medication I had been prescribed, since it contained codeine. I was booked in for Tuesday the following week, and until then I stopped taking the tablets despite the excruciating pain following surgery.

Blessed Assurance

On Tuesday, I went to the physician for my appointment. I told him what I was experiencing, then he examined my stomach and prescribed medication for constipation but nothing changed. I continued to feel constipated and bloated, and by now, my stomach was growing big because of the bloating. It was unbearable. I vomited a lot, and when I did, it was the only time I felt better. At night I could not sleep because of the pain, and I was growing weak from lack of food as I had no appetite to eat; whenever I did eat, I vomited.

It continued for the next five days, and on the fifth day I could not take it anymore. My stomach was swollen, and I could not eat anything, nor could I vomit anymore. I decided to take a walk outside around the complex. I did two rounds, then I chose to sit in the car to rest for a few minutes. Once there, I drifted into thinking about this chapter. Where was the Holy Spirit while I was going through such pain and bewilderment, not knowing what was happening to me and how it would stop? For days I had been praying and hoping for a miracle, but nothing had changed. When was the Holy Spirit going to whisper to me and show me a way out of this terror?

I started questioning what I had written in this chapter because I felt like He was far away from me at that moment; but while still struggling with my thoughts, a way was provided. A neighbour drove into the compound, and I remembered her mother was a registered nurse. I tried to call her, but when the phone was not answered another thought entered my mind: I decided to just go to the hospital. I could not go alone so I called my brother-in-law, but he was far away and wouldn't be able to get to my place for an hour or so. That seemed too late for me, so I decided to call another

Finding the Holy Spirit's Comfort

friend who lived close to me – but he couldn't get to me quickly either. They ended up arriving at the same time, at which point they had to call an ambulance because my situation had deteriorated drastically.

At the hospital, we had a problem because I had a hospital plan for medical aid, which I could only use after admission; before that, I had to pay cash as an outpatient. I did not have the money at that time and nor did my brother-in-law, so my friend ended up footing the bill for me. After the X-ray, I was approved for admission. It turned out that my small intestines had been perforated in three different areas during the laparoscopy, but the physician had either neglected to tell me or he had not noticed what he had done.

Now, as I look back, the Holy Spirit was with me all along. I was sustained by His power from the day of the laparoscopy to that day I grappled over questions and doubts about His presence. I know for sure that it was He who prompted the thought of going to the hospital and He made it such that my brother-in-law would not come first before my friend because neither of us had money for the preadmission tests. God is so marvellous! I went on to be operated on the following day to sew together the holes on the intestines, and I stayed in ICU for fourteen days and then in the general ward for an additional ten days. I have now fully recovered from the ordeal, all thanks to our living God.

I repeat again, one must stay alert to recognize the way of escape provided already by the Lord. Alone we cannot succeed in following through on the right course; we need the Holy Spirit to make the right choice. Therefore, we should always keep our vertical connection with God active.

We moved from South Africa to the United Kingdom in December 2020, narrowly avoiding travel restrictions and local lockdown regulations, for which we are thankful to God. Recently, while driving back from Birmingham where I had gone for an interview, my mobile phone's battery ran out of power so I could not use GPS. Without that functionality, I drove around in circles, not knowing where I was going. My efforts to follow the road signs were fruitless; at one point, I got on the right road but I was headed in the wrong direction. I began to feel agitated as I glanced at my petrol gauge going down; it was evident that I was hopelessly lost. Eventually, I managed to stop at a shop and buy a USB to charge my phone, after which I finally found my way home.

This incident got me thinking about the Holy Spirit's purpose as our internal guide and daily companion. You see, the road signs are a general guide or reminder for someone who knows the area already. But I needed something specifically tailored for me – in other words, a *personal* guide, like the GPS, to tell me at every point which way to go. In our spiritual journey, we need such personal guidance, which can only come from the Holy Spirit. We may have general advice from other people, or we may even study the Bible, but without the Holy Spirit to interpret the Scriptures, there would not be the spark to turn the words into a living Word. The Bible would end up being like any other book, nursing our feelings for a while but severely lacking long-lasting, transforming power to impact our lives.

Helpful Nuggets

1. The Holy Spirit is equal to Jesus and He is a person.
2. Comfort always begins on the inside, from the Holy Spirit.

3. We must stay alert to recognize the way of escape provided already by the Lord from every temptation.

Chapter Eight

Birth

Abba, Father, all things are possible unto thee; take away this cup from me: nevertheless not what I will, but what thou wilt.

Mark 14:36

After the week we had been given to go and decide whether to abort our baby had passed, we went back to the hospital. We told the physicians that we were not going to terminate the pregnancy. We had decided to allow nature to take its course.

They respected our resolve even though they were sceptical and remarked that the baby might not reach full term and, even if she managed that, she had a limited chance of surviving even for a day given her condition.

And so we continued with the pregnancy until the day my wife went into labour. By the time we eventually arrived at the hospital, my wife was exhausted and drained from the pain which overwhelmed every inch of her body. It seemed she had accepted her fate as she wrestled no more.

The guard knew precisely what he had to do; he promptly brought a wheelchair and whisked my wife to the labour ward. I followed behind, trying hard to keep up for fear of getting lost.

Birth

I was unfortunately stopped from entering the room my wife was taken to for delivery, because the bag with the baby's clothes was too big. Instead, I sat on a nearby bench in the passage feeling heartbroken for the second time. I had failed to witness the birth of my first child, but this time around I had determined to be there, especially given the medical diagnosis we had received – but again it was not meant to be.

Sitting there, I started notifying my relatives that my wife had gone into labour. They were excited and relieved about the news. We had all suffered from feelings of apprehension, but now the much-awaited day had arrived.

Saturday, 28th November, 2015 was really a blessed day, because when I texted my brother-in-law I also received exciting news from him: his wife had gone into labour too. So, we were now expecting two baby girls that day.

About an hour later, I was asked to come and see my wife and baby. I felt overwhelmed with joy and gladness as I bounced off the bench. My wife's ordeal was over now; she was spent, but she had emerged victoriously.

They had put the baby in a separate room because the oxygen equipment was not working correctly in her room. I went to the room where they had put the baby, and there she was, our beautiful and precious daughter. Getting her here had been a tremendous challenge. It was as if we had ventured on to a road entrenched by snares and hurdles, and we'd had to battle our way to this point. Our only weaponry had been our faith in God and our hope for a miraculous ending to the horrendous journey. It was all we needed for assured victory versus the enemy.

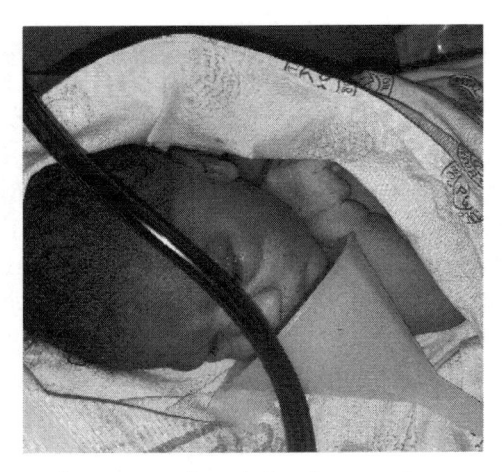

Avery on the night she was born

Avery looked so sweet on that first night. She was also quite big, weighing 2.5 kgs. I checked her to determine if there were any physical anomalies on her body as the doctors had suggested. She had an extra finger on both thumbs, and there was something else that the scans had missed: her stomach did not close completely, making a part of her intestines protrude outside. My heart melted for her. I felt overwhelmed with love and sympathy for her.

I did not lose hope that day. If she was still alive, there was hope for another miracle. It was already a miracle that she had survived termination, reached full-term and everything had gone well to this point – what could go wrong now? I continued with my prayers and fasting as we waited for the confirmation of the heart condition.

It was her second day of fighting for survival, and the battlefield was now in the ICU. Avery was moved there for close monitoring. Her protruding intestines had been tacked in and the wound dressed neatly with a bandage wrapped around her stomach. She was being given extra oxygen. She opened her eyes occasionally, but she kept them shut most of the time. She kept on moving her mouth and tongue as if she were signalling her cravings for milk. Unfortunately, she could not be breastfed until her stomach closed.

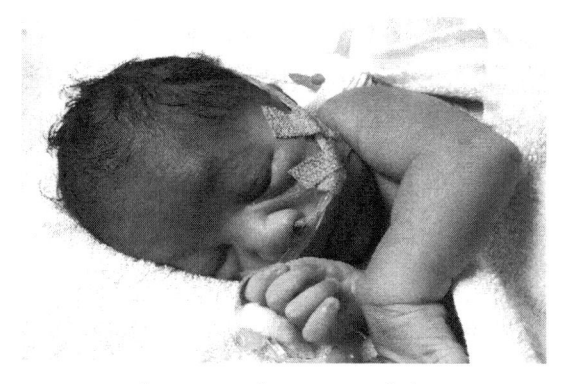

Avery on her second day

I was happy I got a chance to be with her and play with her for most of her second day. It was an awesome experience, but my heart was especially moved when she let out the first cry I heard from her. It was a tiny and weak cry, as though she had been fighting for her life for a long time without any help coming her way. I was moved; how I wished I could trade places with her. The agony seemed too much for her. What crime had she committed that warranted such a high price? Why was she going through such torment alone? Why did it have to be her bearing this burden? This felt so unfair, so unacceptable! These thoughts and questions ran through my mind, demanding answers and explanations.

I left the hospital early that day because I had to take my aunt to the airport. My wife remained behind; she had taken up residence at the hospital. At least someone was there for the baby just in case something was to happen.

It had instantly become a routine: on Avery's third day, I woke up early without waiting for my alarm to go off. I could not wait to be at the hospital with my precious daughter. When I arrived, I found that things had taken a negative turn during the night. She had experienced breathing difficulties, and they'd had to place her on a ventilator to assist her. My baby could no longer get enough oxygen on her own. I was also told that the head of the paediatric ICU wanted to see us, along with the paediatric cardiology department head.

They came just after nine in the morning, and we were summoned into an office. My heart was pounding as I was not sure what they wanted to inform us about.

First, it was the head of the paediatric cardiology department who addressed us. He explained to us extensively what was happening with our child and why it was affecting her breathing. The valve that helps a baby breathe while still in the womb had begun to close, while the iota and the left ventricle were not functioning correctly. He explained that there was no use in intervening and delaying the hole from closing, since they would not do any operation on the baby.

That was hard – *awfully* hard – for me to take, but I had to brave it. There was nothing I could do now except hope for something – just some heavenly intervention, maybe.

The paediatric ICU head then clarified that the baby was on the ventilator in order to give us a chance to say goodbye. They wanted to follow protocol and allow us to have closure with the baby before disconnecting the ventilator, since

Birth

nothing further could be done for her. They wanted to save the ventilator for other children who had a better chance at survival. The ward had only eight ventilators at the time.

I was devastated by the news and could not swallow what I had just heard. I just couldn't accept it. Emotionally, it felt like having something stuck in your throat that you just can't get down. It would take time for the feelings to settle.

They had explained everything beforehand and had warned us about what was now taking place. Some fears are worse in your imagination than in reality – but at other times the reality can be worse than you feared. Even though I had solemnly believed I could handle any situation, this was not what I had expected. I was not prepared for this. A reality was setting in which was the opposite to what I had envisioned and desperately wanted. In my mind, I had thought that somehow God was going to do something about this; he was going to perform a spectacular miracle and heal my baby instantly. I was in denial regarding any other possibility.

Even though I had declared that I was willing to let nature take its course, I was secretly desiring and praying for things to take *my* course. I was convinced I knew the way things should be. They should be *my* way! I had claimed I would always submit to God's will, but what I subconsciously did not mention was the hidden clause: "as long as God's will tallies with mine". God is our Father, but that does not mean we can treat him like our earthly father. We still must reverence Him; that is why the Lord's Prayer is structured the way it is. He is our Father, yes, but His abode is in the heavens and His name is sacred. We need to remember that. The prayer reminds us that *God's* will must be done on earth as well as in heaven – not mine or anyone else's. Yet I could not reconcile myself to what was transpiring at that time. Despite knowing whose will must and would prevail, I still hung on to what I believed should happen. I felt betrayed and cheated!

I remembered the many times in the Bible that God delivered his servants out of terrible situations. *If He could do that for them,* I thought, *He can do it for me. God had the power then and still has the same power now.* But then I thought about how God didn't *always* physically deliver His people. When John the Baptist was arrested and sent messengers to Jesus, Jesus demonstrated His healing power in answer to John's inquiry (Luke 7:19-23), yet He left John in prison only to be beheaded later. We know that on the eve of his execution, Peter slept while the church prayed for his release, and he miraculously escaped, whereas James, the church's first head, was captured and beheaded while the church was praying for him to be set free.

With all this knowledge about God and how He has operated in the past, surely, if He would let my baby die, it must be for a greater purpose. There must be a reason why He should permit it to happen that way. There was some character development needed and some trust issues to be resolved. And someone needed to know their place in the Master / servant relationship.

I requested that the ICU department manager would give us until Friday that week before they would unplug the ventilator, in order to provide our parents time to come and say goodbye to their granddaughter. To my surprise, the manager was very understanding and honoured our request without further questions.

As soon as I reached home, I made phone calls. I organized for our mothers to travel the next day from Zimbabwe to

Birth

South Africa. My father could not come because his passport had expired. I also contacted our church elder, asking him to invite our pastor to assist us with prayers at the hospital. He could not reach our local pastor as he had travelled out of the country; however, the elder managed to arrange with the district pastor to come and assist us.

On Tuesday morning, the district pastor and one of his colleagues arrived at the hospital. We made a special request for them to be allowed in the ICU, as normally only parents of the baby or grandparents were allowed in. Once with Avery, they did not waste any time and started praying for the baby, committing her to the hands of the Lord. I was relieved they had joined us, and I still hoped for a miracle to occur.

The pastor also consoled and comforted us. He said, "At some point, we all die. Each of us has a date on the calendar. We are all going to die; however, we die at different points in life. Some die early, and some in their old age. View it like this: our lives are like ropes; we each get different lengths. Some have short ropes, while others have long ropes. Once you arrive at the end of your rope, it means you have lived in full the life marked for you. And it is not for us to determine who gets what or who doesn't."

This sat well with me. He had answered some of the questions that were racing through my head. Was this by divine providence? Was the Holy Spirit working through him to reach me?

I had wondered why my baby had had to die before me, let alone before even living her life. I had also wondered, *why her*? And now, the pastor was providing answers to my questions. Avery's rope was shorter than mine and anyone else's in the family, and it was the Lord who had allowed it to be that way.

Another thought came into my mind as I was processing this valuable insight: Avery's was an exceptionally long rope after all, considering the rough journey we had travelled to get her to where she was now. She had escaped death many times while in the womb. She was a child disallowed while she was in her mother's womb, but God loved her and had protected her against all odds. A provision for her protection had already been established even before she was formed in her mother's womb. The dream made sure that I would make the right choice when the question to terminate arose. The physicians had predicted that she would not make it to term, but she did. They had indicated that she would not last a day. However, they rushed to put her on a ventilator in our absence and in the presence of God. We had asked for an extension, and they had agreed without question. All of this, I believe, was made possible by divine intervention.

This little girl had escaped death so many times in her short life. The Lord had been with her all this time. I thought she was going through this all alone, but He was sustaining her. Avery's life had been riddled with so many miracles that I could not appreciate before because of my one-dimensional thinking. Nonetheless, we will all die at some point regardless of how many miracles are performed to preserve our lives. That is just the way it is. Jesus resurrected Lazarus from the grave, but Lazarus still died again.

It is my hope that in reading this you will understand that the Lord is always with His children. There are many death traps that He has rescued us from, there are so many sicknesses that He has healed us and our loved ones from, but one day we all have to say goodbye to this world.

The Holy Spirit worked in me through His revelations to me personally and through the pastor's explanations and consoling words. They helped me to better comprehend what had been happening all this time. We need to be open to counselling from individuals sent by God to touch our lives. When we receive the counsel, it must transform us and not just soothe and nurse our feelings for that moment. We need to take decisive action and cut off all wrong views when the proper perspective is revealed. A correct mindset builds you up and draws you closer to God. Anything else that threatens to take you away from His presence must be discarded.

Our parents arrived on Thursday morning, and I went with them to the hospital in the afternoon. I was relieved to have company now at home, since my wife was still staying at the hospital. I also knew that they could handle practical arrangements such as the funeral if Avery were to die.

At the hospital, my wife still could not breastfeed our baby directly; she used a bottle to feed her. Avery now couldn't make any sound while crying. We could see that she was in distress, but no sound was audible; her eyes were closed very tightly as though sealed by her tears. She was exhausted!

Helpful Nuggets

1. God's will must be done – not ours or anyone else's.
2. If God allows suffering, it is for a greater purpose.
3. We need to take decisive action and cut ourselves off from all wrong views when the proper perspective is revealed.

Chapter Nine

Unplugged?

> *For the Lord himself shall descend from heaven with a shout, with the voice of the archangel, and with the trump of God: and the dead in Christ shall rise first: Then we which are alive and remain shall be caught up together with them in the clouds, to meet the Lord in the air: and so shall we ever be with the Lord. Wherefore comfort one another with these words.*
>
> 1 Thessalonians 4:16-18

On Friday, early in the morning, I received a phone call from our local church pastor to inform us that he was now back in the country and that he was available to come along with us to the hospital. This thrilled me since it meant one more opportunity for prayers from a man of God that my daughter would be healed.

My hope for things to gravitate toward my will was still reasonably high, for the Lord may seem slow in answering prayer but is in fact never late. I had learned that from Lazarus' death in John 11. Mary and Martha had thought the only way Jesus Christ could heal their brother would be to come during his illness. Little did they know that Lazarus' death was allowed for a divine purpose higher than anything they could possibly imagine. Jesus, the Resurrection and the Life, referred to Lazarus' death as mere 'sleep' which Lazarus only needed to be awakened from – profound words from Jesus that we can only believe if we are spiritual – and then He proceeded to raise Lazarus from the dead.

We arrived at the hospital together with our parents and the pastor at approximately nine o'clock in the morning. We took turns to see the baby to avoid overcrowding the ward.

I marvelled at one grandmother who had come to see her grandchild in the bed opposite Avery's in the paediatrics ICU. She was busy gazing and admiring our daughter and later commented that she was big and light in complexion and so beautiful. If only she knew how much torment and anguish that body was subjected to and that that day could be her last. If only she knew there was something gruesome and more deadly than what met the eye. Her grandchild had been born prematurely and was so tiny that she could fit in a pocket. Overwhelmed by her granddaughter's condition, the grandmother failed to realize that this tiny child had a better survival outlook than our own daughter.

So often, we admire other people and their seemingly altogether lives based on our superficial observations, and we cut ourselves up with envy and jealousy. Yet beneath the surface, those people we esteem so highly, if they are not Christians, are worse off than us when it comes to things that really matter in life – nonmaterial things; things that are spiritual and are allocated by God. These people may be spending sleepless nights tossing and turning, anxious about tomorrow, worrying about their relationships and all the other insecurities that come with neglecting to store one's "treasures in heaven where neither moth nor rust doth corrupt, and where thieves do not break through nor steal" (Matthew 6:20).

When the ward manager arrived, we were taken to another private room for counselling and to talk through Avery's care. There was virtually no further help they could give to our child, and at the time, I was not financially able to transfer my daughter to a private hospital. That was yet another blow. I blamed myself for some time for not being organized enough to foresee these financial issues. In every situation, the accuser finds a way in that he can use to snare and trap us in order to overthrow and destroy us. This time he used blame and guilt to shift my attention from the Lord and on to myself. Yet I know that no matter how prepared I may have been or how much I would have planned, it is only the Lord who is my enabler. If I do things outside of His will, no matter how meticulous, they will only be like broken cisterns. I could not add a single second to my life by worrying – but there I was, doing it still. I needed help!

After the counselling session, we went back to the ward, and there they finally unplugged our child from the ventilator. They had told us that by taking her off the ventilator, she would not die instantly. Some would take a few hours and some more than a day. The exact time of her death only the Lord would know.

They transferred the baby from the paediatrics ICU ward and placed her on another ward. There they built a small private place for us using curtains.

Though full of pain and apprehension, our journey so far could not compare with our experience now as we watched our baby slowly reach the end of her life. Not knowing how long this would take made it even harder. How do we wait for her to die? How could we be subjected to this torture – watching someone you love dearly slowly ebb away, never to be seen again until the resurrection morning? Nevertheless, I still cleaved to hope. I still thought my baby would get well, even though we were standing there watching her die. I felt that, just like Jairus' daughter, her spirit was going to be revived and she was going to be healed instantly. I had fasted and prayed for her healing for three months. Something had to happen. I kept repeating the words of Jesus in Luke 8:50 where He said to Jairus, "Fear not: believe only, and she shall be made whole."

My baby, I believed, was also going to be made whole. For her sake, I had to have faith, didn't I? While growing up, my worst fear was the death of loved ones. I would never have believed that I would be able to handle the death of someone so dear to me. I was possessive towards my loved ones, which I now believe was anchored in selfishness. My underlying problem at that time, as I now know, was fear of rejection and someone dying; I translated it as them giving up on me. At one time as a young boy, I think around ten years old, I prayed a series of prayers to God that I would be able to share all my remaining years with my loved ones: my parents, my siblings and my only living grandparent at the time, my mother's mother. During those times, my fear was intense. A family member getting ill used to terrify me because I would be thinking that they are now dying. If tragedy were to happen, I reasoned, it had to happen to me and not to them.

I realized that my prayer had not been answered when my grandmother died. It was horrific, but I was able to handle it better than I thought I would. However, the fear did not really go away, because of my selfishness, even though I was now a committed Christian. I had not yet handed over the throne of my life to God; I was still sitting there.

Now my daughter's eyes were completely shut. She no longer showed any sign of crying, just an occasional movement of her lips and legs. Without the many tubes that had been taped on her face, we could now see her clearly; even though she was in such agony, she still maintained a beautiful countenance. She was not resisting the course of nature; she completely accepted her fate, and she did not know anything else besides her trauma. Her contentment with pain only indicated the sustenance of the Lord.

We started taking turns to pray for her. The pastor's presence meant so much to me. He had arrived in South Africa and had come straight to us in his jeans. He apologized for his casual clothing, but how he dressed did not matter; it only confirmed his love and empathy for the individuals in his congregation as he had rushed straight to see us. That day was my first time talking to him personally, but we were part of God's sheep in his care; hence, he came regardless.

He was not dressed for church, but he delivered the best possible sermon for my family, including our mothers, just by his presence the whole day. He could have been elsewhere more pressing for him, but he chose to cancel all his other plans for the day to be with his grieving and sorrowful people. To think that our only connection was the church makes one marvel. Our parents later commended his care, dedication and duty to others. They had never seen such love and unity lived out.

At approximately four o'clock in the afternoon, we had another round of prayers. When the last person was still praying, my wife saw that our baby girl had gone into cardiac arrest. The oxygen monitor started beeping very loud, but no help came. My wife panicked as the reality of what was happening crushed her. She ran to get someone to come and assist our daughter, forgetting why we had been waiting a whole day. This was supposed to happen; we were waiting for nature to take its course, there was nothing further that the hospital could provide us with.

My pastor broke down into tears as he was hammered by reality. There was a sombre atmosphere as if a heavy, dark cloud had been dropped from heaven. I rushed to pick my child up into my arms, then I broke into a prayer; there was still a chance, I felt, the sun could shine for her yet. This baby had to go home with us, my heart shouted, not this other home she was crossing over to. A miracle had to happen! So I prayed. I just could not lose her. No, not yet!

Suddenly, she stabilized again as her oxygen levels started to rise. I held her for a while longer before I put her back on her bed.

After the scare, the gloominess and despondency had intensified; we no longer knew what to do. We did not know if there would be another cardiac arrest, or whether Avery would simply slip away, or whether she would come back to us, ready to go home and experience the life we had imagined for her. I couldn't help but think about how on the day she was born I could not be in the labour room because of the bag of clothes we had brought for her, and now that she lay there dying without ever having worn a single item in that bag.

I shifted my attention to the pastor. I greatly admired him that day as he sympathized with us. The tears from his eyes touched me. They were genuine; he felt the pain that we were going through even though he didn't have children of his own.

Sometimes no words are necessary to comfort someone; simply your presence and authentically sharing someone's sorrows and pain is enough. The message you share just by your company may surpass what you could ever put into words. Let us be there for one another.

I was reminded of Jesus after Lazarus died. The Bible says, "Jesus wept" (John 11:35). And on another occasion he cried for Jerusalem (Matthew 23:37). Jesus allowed Himself to be touched by the plights of humanity, just as our pastor did now. Even though those who die while Christians are merely sleeping in Christ ready to wake on the resurrection morning, we still weep and mourn for them, but our weeping and mourning are different from those who are not connected to God. For us, there is a solution to our weeping and our mourning. We have assurance, comfort and hope in Jesus, who is the resurrection and the life, and who will one day come back to awaken those who are sleeping. On that great day, the resurrection morning, both those who have died and those still living will meet him in the skies. We must share this wonderful hope with those deprived of this message by the devil.

The pastor left around five o'clock that evening. He had spent nearly the whole day with us at the hospital. This was a huge sacrifice. Our pastor's presence that day ministered to us and affected transformation in us, drawing us nearer to God's throne, as had the two pastors who came earlier in the week. His demonstration of love and self-sacrifice drew us closer to God more than his sermons in the pulpit ever had.

As you minister to others, you also get ministered to. That is how we grow; no one is ever a finished product. We are disciples as we disciple others; I am sure that while God used the pastor to preach to us, He also used Avery to touch the pastor. I am sure that the condition he witnessed at the hospital made a lasting impact on his life. Avery's story is to be incorporated in his sermons as he continues with the furtherance of God's Word.

After he left, we remained only a short while, as it was already time to go home – yet Avery was still alive. My wife came back home with us for the first time as she was now exhausted and could not feed the baby anymore.

Helpful Nuggets

1. The things that really matter in life are spiritual and are allocated by God.
2. Sometimes no words are needed to comfort someone; just our presence and genuinely sharing their sorrows and grief is enough.
3. As we minister to others, we also get ministered to. That is how we grow; no one is ever a finished product.

Chapter Ten

Avery's Legacy

Beloved, think it not strange concerning the fiery trial which is to try you, as though some strange thing happened unto you: But rejoice, inasmuch ye are partakers of Christ's sufferings; that, when his glory shall be revealed, ye may be glad also with exceeding joy.

1 Peter 4:12-13

Her assignment here was strange, but the message of her life was loud and clear; it was a message of love and self-sacrifice. Avery, like Paul, fought a good fight, finished her course, kept the faith, and now it was time for her to depart; she was ready to be offered up.

When we got home from the hospital, I checked my phone and saw missed calls from the hospital. Avery had reached the end of her life on this earth. The nurse confirmed she had died a few minutes after we had left the hospital. Our Avery slept in Christ!

The news crushed my spirit. It was hard to contemplate. We had waited the whole day for that possibility and yet I had still hoped for a miracle. I thought about all my fasting and prayers. Was there a possibility that I did not do enough?

Avery's Legacy

What did I do wrong? Again, I had a lot of questions without answers.

I conveyed the news to the pastor. "Our heroine is no more," I mumbled, unable to say more. I felt weak in the knees as the reality of the situation became clear; she was not coming home. All that was left was for us to join her someday.

After speaking to the pastor, I went into the living room. It did not feel like a living room anymore as I entered. All eyes were on me as they waited for me to confirm what had happened. "Avery has left us," I said flatly.

The news stabbed at them; the tears that were teetering suddenly broke out. No one could hold them in any longer. Everyone cried silently as we came to terms with the news.

My wife and I woke up early the following morning; we searched for a funeral parlour to arrange for cremation. We found one in Pretoria, and they said they would process the paperwork on Monday. That was when we would collect her body from the mortuary and perhaps see her for the last time.

When we arrived home on that Saturday after making these arrangements, our fellow brothers and sisters in Christ came to conduct an afternoon service at our home, but our pastor was not available because of an engagement elsewhere. The elder who stood in his place spoke on 2 Samuel 12:16-24 where David fasted and prayed for his son, petitioning God to have mercy on him and spare the child from dying. This had been the very story I had been modelling when I fasted and prayed for my daughter. The elder's emphasis was on the last part of the passage when, after the child's death, David started eating and worshipped God. This was the real miracle: that David did not lose heart and did not refuse to eat after the end of the child's life; neither did he make it a reason to stop worshipping his God and make the devil pleased. David clung to his Lord because he knew God chastises those He loves; he knew everything other than God was sinking ground for him.

The preacher emphasized that we should emulate David and act likewise, and he encouraged us not to forsake our Lord because of the tragedy. As David acknowledged, the child was not coming back to us, but someday we would join our child.

Here again, God was using someone else to reach me. God had a message for me in that story. That is why the Holy Spirit preciously brought it to my memory, and now He was graciously using someone else to reiterate the message, stopping me being drawn away from God's message by pain and despondency.

Even though, like in David's case, God allowed the tragedy to happen, it did not mean that he had forsaken us. Just as He later blessed David and Bathsheba with another baby, Solomon, we too were blessed with a rainbow baby, a healthy boy, two years later.

The following morning, our pastor came to give us counsel and pay his respects. He advised me not to suppress my feelings toward God. I had to allow myself to ask all the questions I had and to express any anger I felt against Him. Even as I questioned Him, I knew that He loved me and He would listen and give the answers I was seeking. Our pastor also reassured us that Avery was going to go to heaven on the resurrection morning. Avery's place in heaven was guaranteed for her, since she died an innocent baby without sinning against anyone. The choice was left for us as parents to secure our own place in heaven and so be reunited with Avery one day. We had to live our lives as those who had accepted Jesus Christ as our Lord and Saviour. We were not to allow anything to hinder us or derail us from traveling along that heaven-bound straight and narrow path.

This was yet another consolation and fortification; I heard God reaching out to me through His servant. He answered one of the persistent questions which had been reverberating around in my head. I had repeatedly asked myself what my dream really meant. I had been told that I would not lack or lose anything but I had just lost a baby. Was it a paradox or even some form of mockery? But now, the pastor brought clarity into my life. He lightened the burden on me by sharing that I had not really lost my baby but gained her. If Avery's place in heaven was secured, then I was guaranteed one of my children would be there, and it was up to me now to make sure that my place there was secured as well. I had one more joy in heaven to anticipate. As well as knowing the love of God, I now had something else to go to heaven for.

The days following Avery's death were saturated with many reflections and revelations as I sought to reconcile all the sorrow with the enlightening experiences that had befallen us since the day of the dream. I had a cocktail of questions that God had to provide answers for. As days went by, however, things started to fall into place.

Before our daughter's death, my wife and I lived a fairly private life. We hardly fellowshipped with other church members. We routinely visited the church, listened to the preacher and then left as soon as the service ended. At times we would not even return for the afternoon service. There was no time to socialize and build meaningful connections with other families. That soon changed after the death of our child. It was amazing how things altered dramatically because of the woe that had come. Out of the bitter calamity, something sweet emerged. Some of the church's loving members took a keen interest in us and began inviting and encouraging us to stay for the potluck lunch and participate in church programmes. We got involved and made family friends with other church members. Very soon our Sabbaths were enriched; we stepped up our attendance and looked forward to each Lord's Day. We stopped missing church like we had sometimes done previously, because we felt like we were now part of the church family. We even went on to hold positions of responsibility in our congregation. I know that the magnitude of the spiritual growth and change in our lives would not have been so great had we terminated the pregnancy. God has His own way of making things beautiful in the end; therefore, we ought to trust and obey Him always.

Helpful Nuggets

1. When we have suffered great loss, we should not turn our back on God. Everything other than God is sinking ground.
2. In times of trouble, God can reach us through the comfort and counsel of his servants around us.
3. With God, out of bitter calamity, something sweet can emerge. God has His own way of making things beautiful in the end.

CHAPTER ELEVEN

Did God Answer Our Prayers?

Call unto me, and I will answer thee, and shew thee great and mighty things, which thou knowest not.
                                                     Jeremiah 33:3

It could have seemed to us that our prayers had not been answered. Even as Christians we can sometimes find ourselves perplexed when our prayers do not lead to the expected outcomes. We can start wondering, "Is it that I don't have enough faith, or is it something I have done? Is there something wrong with me or does God have something against me? Why is it that prayer does not seem to work for me?"

However, truly prayer *does* grab the attention of God and can even change His mind, as Scripture testifies. In your own life as well, maybe you can remember times when you got on your knees and evoked God's name in faith and got the attention of heaven. It could have been an intercessory prayer petitioning God to heal someone or to stop something from happening that you had been shown in a vision or dream.

I remember one striking and unforgettable day – 29th September, 2002 – when God heard my prayer and answered immediately. I had previously attended an interview for apprentice training at Air Zimbabwe Training School. We had a written interview, and the pass mark was seventy percent. I scored eighty-one percent on that interview and I was so ecstatic. "I have made it!" I exclaimed to myself. One of the other interview candidates turned out to be my uncle. I was happy to know there was a relative of mine there already. Upon going home, we were told that we would receive confirmation letters informing us when we would start training within two weeks.

I went home very pleased with myself. When I arrived, some two hundred and sixty-five kilometres away, my parents were happy to receive the news. Everyone was so proud of me.

Days went by and the confirmation never came. One day, my father returned from work and informed me that my uncle had already received his confirmation letter and would go on 29th September, 2002. Since I resided in a remote area, postal parcels took longer to arrive, so I decided to call the training school for confirmation. I explained to the manager why I thought I had not yet received my letter, and he briskly asked me to hold on while he crosschecked on the spreadsheet to see if I had passed. He came back to inform me that I had passed and I was supposed to join the others on 29th September.

When the day arrived, we assembled in the lecture theatre for a brief welcome, and after this the manager began collecting our consent letters. Only I didn't have one. The manager was not happy, and after questioning me and finding out what had happened, he informed me that I had not got a good enough grade to be accepted on the course.

"How do you mean, sir?" I queried. "The pass mark was seventy percent, and I had eighty-one percent. Also, on the phone you confirmed to me that I had passed and informed me to come here this day."

Did God Answer Our Prayers?

"OK," he explained, "after the students left on the day of the interviews, we discovered that so many people had passed that we increased our pass mark to ninety-five percent for boys and eighty percent for girls. You can check for yourself." He lowered the spreadsheet in my direction. "Look, here is your name way down here, and our ticks ended up here. You see here where there is a tick? This was the last person we took with ninety-five percent. So how can I leave this one with ninety-four percent and take you with just eighty-one percent?" he asked.

That was his first mistake. He gave me a chance to give him a reason to take me despite my failure!

"Well, sir, there is the justification of what I was told on the phone. Secondly, that person with ninety-four percent is not here because he does not belong here. I am here because I belong here. It's the power of being present." I pointed out the reasons assuredly, remembering the many hours I had spent in my school days reading books on self-development.

Still he refused vehemently to let me stay, but he made another mistake by giving me an option to stick around a bit longer with the other students.

So, I chose to stay, and joined the rest of the prospective students. The other students looked excited and curious as they learned about aircraft; in the meanwhile, I was wondering how matters were going to end. How was I going to face my parents and the girl who was my girlfriend at the time? I had been so proud when I had informed her about all I was going to do. Now I dreaded going back and telling her that it was all a mistake and I had actually failed the interview.

A little while later, when all the other new students had been allocated to their classrooms, again, it was just him and me left in the lecture theatre. He urged me to go home but gave me the option of allowing me to stay in the lecture hall until I was ready to leave. That was the third mistake he had made that day – I chose to remain glued to my seat.

As soon as he left the room, I broke into a silent prayer, asking God to intervene and rescue me from the precarious situation I found myself in. I made many promises to God that I would fulfil if He would just let me have that opportunity! Before I could say amen, the manager was back again.

"Ah, young man. You are still here?" he asked, not expecting an answer. "You are fortunate," he exclaimed. "Can you start next month? Do you have someone to pay your school fees? We need to fill the class for October this year."

"Yes, I am willing; my father can pay the fees," I responded ecstatically. Apparently, three people on the list had not turned up on that day.

"OK, follow me. You are a fighter, young man, a bull!" He now complimented me with appreciation.

Imagine what would have happened had I given up too early. I would have faced the humiliation of telling my girlfriend and my other friends that it had been a mistake; I had not made it. Many a time, we give up in life when we are on the verge of a breakthrough. This must never be you! At each juncture, I was given a glimmer of hope which I held on to each time. The hand of God was there all along. All this divine providence enlisted my participation. It's not that God cannot work and do everything alone; rather, He encourages community and fosters interdependency among humans in partnership with Him.

In the case of our prayers for Avery, however, we did not give up – our prayers were not answered in the way we

Did God Answer Our Prayers?

expected, but God was doing something different. God always knows how to give good gifts to His children, and the gifts He gives last forever – like the living water Jesus spoke of that, having drunk it, you never thirst again. He provides for our momentary needs, but He is more into the business of transforming our characters in preparation for heaven. In retrospect, I can see that in His tender, loving mercy, God answered our prayers before we knew we would ever need Him. Before the impending heart-breaking journey and subsequent death of our child that we would face, He had already stepped in. The stones in my dream represented the assurance given to me that after receiving and upholding God's words, I would not lose anything. The certainty that God will fulfil all His promises towards us is a blessed assurance indeed. As Paul writes about Jesus in 2 Corinthians 1:20, "For all the promises of God in him are yea, and in him Amen, unto the glory of God by us." This is a source of comfort and hope, whatever trials and griefs we face in life.

It is truly a blessing to have this deep assurance, rooted in the Word of God. Although we didn't fully grasp this during our journey, and our prayers were often misplaced, focusing on what we wanted rather than recognising what God was doing in our lives, God was faithful towards us and never abandoned us. He used the events of this book to prune us in order that we would become even more fruitful for Him and for His glory. He allowed suffering in order to prepare us for eternity – to be changed "from glory to glory" (2 Corinthians 3:18), more into the image of Christ.

As for Avery, she was a blessing, and known by heaven even before her birth. Though her brief life seemed to be one of pain and suffering, it was riddled with miracles and sustained by the Lord himself.

Until we fully connect with Jesus and surrender our lives to Him, we cannot know the depths of peace that can be experienced in the midst of pain and suffering. If you have not made that step in your own life yet, I encourage you to turn to Him in prayer now and invite Him into your life.

Helpful Nuggets

1. Our prayers move heaven and they are received by God, even when it seems like the answer we expected does not come.
2. God often encourages us to partner with him in the fulfilment of our prayers.
3. God always knows how to give good gifts to His children, and the gifts He gives last forever

Dedication to Avery

Though your life was as brief as the morning dew, we are forever indebted and thankful to God for it and for the powerful lessons he taught us through it about selflessness, unconditional love and obedience.

About the Author

Simon Makuyana is an author with a ministry passion for teaching and discipleship. Born in Zimbabwe, he served from 2016 to 2020 in a Bible-believing church in South Africa, where his roles included deacon ministry and teaching, as well as running the work for youth aged 16-21. Simon and his family now live in Burntwood, United Kingdom.

To contact Simon, please write to:

Simon Makuyana
c/o Onwards and Upwards Publishers Ltd.
4 The Old Smithy
London Road
Rockbeare
EX5 2EA

More information about the author can be found on the book's web page:

www.onwardsandupwards.org/blessed-assurance